When
OBEYING
GOD
MAKES YOU LOOK
STUPID

When OBEYING GOD MAKES YOU LOOK STUPID

THE STORY OF MY FIDELITY OF FAITH

SHAVON SELLERS

ISBN: 978-1-7341479-0-2 (Paperback)
978-1-7341479-1-9 (E-Book)

Library of Congress Control Number: 2019916035

Front cover image by Prize Publishing House.
Book design by Prize Publishing House.

Printed by Prize Publishing House, in the United States of America.

First printing edition 2019.

Prize Publishing House
P.O. Box 9856
Chesapeake, VA 23321

www.ShavonSellers.org

Contents

Acknowledgements...vii

Foreword...ix

Introduction..xi

Chapter 1   When Your Obedience Doesn't Make
Sense to the Natural Eye 1

Chapter 2   Trusting God when You Can't Trace or
Track Him 10

Chapter 3   Develop an Ear to Hear the
Voice of the Lord............................. 18

Chapter 4   Detaching from Things You
are Attached To...............................27

Chapter 5   Overcoming Fear 32

Chapter 6   Embracing the New 37

Chapter 7   Having Confidence in Taking
New Territory 46

Chapter 8   Trusting that You are not in Trouble
During Transition 55

Conclusion...63

About the Author...73

Acknowledgements

This has been one of the hardest yet most rewarding seasons I have ever experienced, and there have been three individuals who have been my motivation, my pushers, my prayer partners and my reasons to never give up; they are my children, Clarence III, Marlon and Kalyn.

CL (Clarence III), my first born, my businessman; words can't express how dear you are to me. I remember praying before you were born, and God gave me everything I prayed for and more when he gave me you. You help me celebrate every blessing and you know when I am sad even when I try so hard not to let you and your siblings see it. In the darkest season of my life, I remember you coming home to just lay in the bed and love on me and make me laugh. I look at the man that you have become and smile knowing that God gave me such an amazingly loving, God fearing son.

Marlon, my warrior… you are one of the most disciplined and responsible beings that I know. You are a natural born leader, so mild mannered; yet you are so SMOOTH... I sit back in amazement to look at you and reflect on you giving me the "business" when you were a baby... LOL. Now I see a man; a man that I don't have to give orders to more than once; a man that doesn't ask for much and never wants to inconvenience anyone. You are so respectful and loving. I smile when you call me while I am traveling to ensure I'm safe; I smile when I see you get on your knee to pray with your teammates before and after every football game; I smile when you are hanging with your baby sister always making sure she is good. When I think of you son, I always smile.

Kalyn, my princess, my baby. You are literally my mini me. God gave me a real-life doll when he gave me you. Each day, I strive to be a better example for you because I know you are always watching. I pray every day that God protects your heart because it is so tender, and I never want it to become broken. Your love for people is so pure and you will give your absolute last. Every day you make me so proud to be your mother. I am blown away about the young lady you are becoming. You are so creative, so adventurous and so FLY! You may be growing up on me, but you will always be my NaNa, my baby!

Foreword

The incomprehensible challenge of obeying God has made the lives of many great people but a mere classroom, full of the lessons and contemplations that our obedience or the lack thereof taught us. It is with little doubt that scripture shows us that nothing in our observable experience disobeys God quite like humans. The stars, sun, nature, cosmic elements, etc. obediently function in a way that is congruent with God's idea of its purpose. The created world's praise to God is its obedience. Yet, we, the human, find it a challenge.

Created with a will, one of the fundamental differences between humans and other created things is that we are allowed to decide and elect among the various desires we will experience, even those that do not honor God. Life to us is often a pull and tug between a life that follows the throws of congruency with God, and those that do not. Obedience, then, as some would say, is a 'will' issue. It is an issue of making active and sometimes alternative opinions apart from God- and living with the consequences. Since we all have a will, shaped by our unique experiences, a true issue in the Christians' journey is finding harmony between his/her own opinions and God's.

Obeying God is not like following any other instruction, because God pushes, and nags, and pulls the one He loves and trusts. He doesn't bend and is unrelenting when it comes to His purposes. Obedience is at the core the primary demand of God to us. And yet at times, so difficult. Nonetheless, the empowering nature of God gives us enough divine inspiration to find our elusive 'yes' within ourselves to give him our allegiance.

Pastor Shavon's story, is the story of faith, courage, and trust. It is a journey experienced by millions of believers whose greater desire is to honor God and fulfill his will for their life, while at the same time juxtaposing this desire with the opposite intensity developed by other stimuli. Pastor leads the charge reminding us of the humbling, at times humiliating, and most times misunderstood task associated with obeying God. If you thought that you were alone, Pastor Shavon reminds us all, that we are not, there will be times when obeying God make us look stupid!

Enjoy her story and let it bring encouragement to your walk with God!

Dr. Terrell Fletcher
City of Hope International Church, Pastor

Introduction

I've been waiting for the right time to tell this part of my life. And I'm excited because now is definitely the right time. It's really the perfect time, because I am literally in the middle of a major transition in my life.

This transition has pretty much required me to leave and walk away from something that has not been bad *for* me. To walk away from something that has not been a burden *to* me.

It's easy to walk away from things that cause you harm. It's easy to walk away from things that cause you stress. It's easy to walk away from things that may be toxic.

But when it's something *good*, when it's something that is a blessing to you, when it's something that's wholesome - to walk away from *that* is *not* easy.

I'm in a season in my life where I must walk away from a baby that has been birthed. I birthed a ministry three years ago called The Life Center, and this was a center that was established where people could come and really receive new life. They came broken. They came wounded.

If they came addicted to anything, drugs, sexual addiction, emotional sickness, mental sickness - whatever the issue was - this place was established for them to be able to come and receive new life.

In these three years, that is what I've seen take place. People's lives are being transformed. Those that were addicts, those that were addicted to drugs, those that sold drugs, those that served jail time, those that couldn't get jobs, those that couldn't read - I've seen their lives totally transformed.

And yet, three years later at the prime of the ministry, where I feel that finally the *why* I was established is coming to fruition, I hear the voice of God tell me, "It's now time for you to release that life. I'm going to transition you to something else because what you have done here at The Life Center in the city of Portsmouth, Virginia, I need you to take that somewhere else."

The crazy thing is, I don't know where that somewhere else is, as of yet. It's like taking a walk blindfolded. It's walking and really *obeying* God when you don't even know where the next place is.

Talking to people and sharing *just that little bit*, I'm finding that there are so many people in transition as well. While they may not have the *same* story that I'm having about leaving a ministry, these people are in a transition of some type.

And this transition is something that is not *easy,* but it is something that is very necessary. *It's also very scary.* But if you never make a transition, then you will not grow.

Leaving that place of comfort, leaving that place of familiarity is necessary if you want to attain bigger, greater, and more. I just believe that is God's requirement. That in order for Him to *give* you more, you've got to be willing to walk away from where you are.

I don't feel as if this next transition is going to be a place where I will be stuck inside of a building. I was already doing ministry in a church building, here at The Life Center.

This new season in my life is going to be wherever God sends me -

- It might be on a street corner.
- It might be in a nightclub.
- It might be on the basketball court.
- It may even be in a strip club.

God is moving me from out of the box. He is moving me from a place where I will no longer be limited to just the church. *He is releasing me to go to the world.* To serve the same type of people I serve now.

The Life Center was just a glimpse of the type of people that I'm going to be assigned to.

The Life Center is not the typical, traditional church. Most of the church and those that ended up joining and coming into fellowship with the ministry were people that were not church people. Meaning they didn't have a church background; their parents were not brought up in the church.

For some, this is their *first* church experience. For many others, this is their first time even coming into a relationship *with* Jesus Christ. And *that's* who I wanted, that's who I prayed for.

So, I don't feel like the type of people will change. I just believe that God is sending me to make a different impact in a different area.

$\mathcal{T}$EST OF OBEDIENCE

Right now, I am looking *really* crazy to some people. The thing is, this is not my first time. God has tested me in this type of area - of obedience - *several times before*.

When I first came into a greater knowledge of who Jesus is, I prayed. I really wanted to know about the power of God. The church I was raised in was a pretty staunch church, strict in their teachings, and didn't really believe in women doing ministry.

But I always felt a tug. I always felt a call from God to do ministry, so, when I was in high school getting ready to graduate and go into college, I walked away from the church that I grew up in. That was *not* an easy decision because I was still living at home with my mom and dad.

I had to tell them, "Mom and dad, the Lord is telling me that it's time for me to leave and go to another ministry."

This was something that wasn't received well. It wasn't popular, it wasn't understood. *And* I was ridiculed for doing it. I remember my mom crying. I remember them talking with the other members and just saying, "My daughter, we don't know what's going on with her."

They were sad and felt that I was pretty much losing my mind. That I was following whoever. They were so disappointed. It didn't make me feel good to disappoint or hurt them.

But that's when I really built my relationship with the Lord. When I knew what God was instructing me to do. That was when I learned how to obey God even when the people that you love the most don't get it.

I never wanted to be disrespectful to my parents. I wanted their blessings. I asked them, "May I go to another church?"

They gave me their permission which I believe the Lord had already given to them to release me. But I know that they did not understand. It was hurtful. That lasted a while until I got married.

When I got married, they came to visit the church where we were pastoring. That's when they started to see, "She's alright. It didn't turn out the way we thought. We thought that she was turning away from God, but now we understand why she did what she did."

It took them years to really understand why I made the decision I made. Even now for me being a female pastor, my mother still does not embrace that. She never called me a pastor. She has always said that women are not called to do that work.

Whenever she would come to the church, she would say, "You're doing a good work as a missionary. But I would never refer to you as a pastor."

I did what I know God called me to do during that season. It was a thing where I had to respect her feelings. I was not going to allow her to stop me from doing what I'm called to do, but I am still going to respect her as my mother.

If I never made that decision, then I would have never learned about the power of God. I would never have come into the ministry that I know God was calling me for. I would never have been able to travel the nation and be a missionary and share the love of Christ. So *that* happened.

Then, years later I ended up going through a divorce. That was major because I walked away from a marriage of seventeen years. Which also meant walking away from *two* churches that we pastored.

So here we are again. Now, *five* years later I'm at another transition where I am now walking away from The Life Center. I've looked kind of crazy several times. *But*, as it plays out, it will *all* make sense later.

There's no way you are going to live a successful life, a life of impact, a life where you really influence others, if you're not willing to transition.

There's no way that you're going to grow personally if you make yourself stay in the same place. There comes a time where you really outgrow where you are.

You must be honest enough to say, *"The ground that I'm on is no longer able to hold me."*

You are too weighty for where you are. The womb that you have been in - you have outgrown that place. I liken it to a baby inside a mother's womb who has now grown all their limbs. Their legs are developing. Their hands are developing. They have their eyes. They have all their features.

They want to stretch out now, but the womb is no longer large enough for them to do so. So now it's time to come out from that place of warmth. To come out from that place of familiarity. To come out from that place of comfort and security. Now it's time to come out into the world where there are limitless possibilities.

It is the same thing that God is willing to do for many of you that are in transition, but you are afraid of obeying God because you are worried about how it is going to look.

- You are afraid to obey God because you are worried about what people are going to say.
- You are afraid to obey God because you don't know where the resources are going to come from.
- You are afraid to obey God because you don't know who will be on the other side.
- You are afraid to obey God because it is unfamiliar territory.

I *promise* you, God will not require you to leave something - to leave a place, to leave people, to leave a job, to leave a home - **and not give you more than what you leave behind.**

What You Will Learn From This Book

I believe that this message, *this book*, is going to minister or speak to the male *and* the female, as well as anyone who is just going through life. I believe this book is not just for one specific gender, but it's going to be a blessing to anybody that reads it.

We have all had to - in one way or another, at one time or another - face transition. Most likely more than once. And if you haven't, if you live long enough, you *will*. You need to know that this doesn't mean you've done something wrong.

Transition doesn't mean you are in trouble. It just means you are being prepared for something else. You should understand that it is an honor to even be trusted in transition.

To go through a transition and to go through it without backpedaling, you must stay focused on the instructions from the Lord. You have got to follow His instructions to a T.

I liken that unto the life of Abraham. Here is a man that has been established. He's comfortable. He's familiar with his surroundings. He's grown older.

And yet, when he is seventy-five years old, God tells him, "Alright, Abraham, I need you to now leave where you are and go to a land that I'm going to show you."

Abraham had to obey the voice of God and blot out *any* negative voices that would speak opposite of what God told him.

As we're in transition, we must stay true to the instructions that we receive. We can't be distracted by what's going on at the sidelines.

You must have that tunnel vision to tell yourself, "I'm going to a place, I may not know exactly where it is, but I'm following God's instructions, and I *will not* be deterred by what I don't see."

This is where our faith in God comes into play. Faith means, "I don't see it, but I believe it,"

And so, I may not have all the details, but my faith in God says that He is not going to set me up to fail. You must have an ear to hear the voice of God. Have your faith in Him so solid, knowing that as weird as this seems, as uncomfortable as this may be, as unorthodox as it may look, my faith in God is secure.

I know that if God is telling me to do it, that means He is setting me up to win. He is setting me up for victory. He is setting me up to be able to share *this* testimony for somebody else. So, it *looks* bad, but it's going to work out for my good.

Reading This Book

- You will see how strong you are.
- You will be able to realize that there is much more to you than you could ever imagine.
- You will realize what is in you and be able to identify the gifts and talents you fully have and put yourself in a position for those gifts to be manifested.

This transition has shown *me* my strength and how I walk as a woman of independence. *I am a leader.* I am not making decisions based on what people think. I truly have a solid relationship with the Lord, and it shows that my faith in God is at a good place.

This book will show you how your testimony and your life can be a blessing to someone else.

For Someone That Is Questioning

- What will happen if I make that move?
- Will God provide?
- What is on the other side of this?

I believe just watching *me* go through this transition will inspire you to step out, to launch out, to take the risk. Because if you never launch out, if you never step out, if you never *jump* all the way in the water, you will *never* know what you've been missing out on.

Chapter One

WHEN YOUR OBEDIENCE DOESN'T MAKE SENSE TO THE NATURAL EYE

We are what you would say at the prime of our ministry. This ministry is only three years old, but in three years it has grown in a very rapid way. Every time the doors opened people came in from everywhere. From all the cities that circle the city that we're in.

People were coming. There were men coming, there were women coming, and there were families coming. People were being married here. It was almost as if our ministry was put on display for everyone to see. It was the talk of the town.

Pastors were reaching out and asking, "*What* are you doing? How is your church growing so? How is it that you're a single woman and you are winning men in your church? How is it that you are a Black female pastor and you have Caucasian men, women, and couples joining your ministry? *What is it that you're doing that we're not doing?"*

Then I received the award for being the best pastor in the area. So, leaving now doesn't make sense. People are thinking it's very strange that I would leave at this time.

They are saying, "Your ministry is doing well. It's not like you're at a downslope. It's not as if your ministry is declining. You're at a place where your ministry is *the* place people want to come to. And *now* you want to walk away?"

It doesn't add up. It just isn't making *any* sense. There *must be* some other type of reason, right?

People are coming up with their own reasons, "Maybe they're going through some things financially. Maybe it's something that she's not telling. Maybe she's terminally ill. Maybe she's getting ready to get married and she didn't want anyone to know. Maybe something happened inside the church. Maybe there was some type of scandal."

Everyone is coming up with *their* logical reasons, "Her just obeying God – that cannot be the reason why she's walking away from such a great place. From such a great people. This does not make any sense."

I have people questioning my obedience, "Why would God have you to do that? It's not making sense."

More questions of, "What are you going to do? How are you going to survive?"

"What is going to be your livelihood? What is your next move? This does not make sense."

"Why would you just walk away from something when you have nothing else set up? *It does not make any sense.* You *look* stupid."

In transition, you have got to be very careful not to share everything. I've *purposely* shared the details I have because I believe that as people watch the story, it is going to be such a testimony that is going to come out of it. Because where I look now, it doesn't look good. It does look *very* crazy.

But as things unfold, as we see what God has in mind, *then* it's going to be like, "*Wow,* now it all makes sense."

The things that I am sharing and the little details that I do have, I'm sharing them on purpose. Because I want you to walk through this story with me. I know I look crazy, but I want you to *see* me looking crazy. Because I also want you to see the outcome.

God spoke to me when I *first* started The Life Center. This was after my divorce and leaving the churches we pastored. There I was asking the Lord, "What's my purpose? What am I going to do now that I'm not a First Lady anymore? I don't have a place where I'm ministering at churches. All I do now is travel. When I'm not traveling, what church do I go to? Where do *I* belong?"

That is when He put it in my heart to establish The Life Center. When I prayed and asked the Lord how this should be done and what should the name be, God gave me the name and all the details.

He specifically told me, "Shavon, I am going to allow you to do this for three years, and *after* the three years pass, then I am going to shift you."

Well, that was three years ago, so I heard it. I received it.

I said, "Okay, God," and I got excited. I'm working in the church. I'm building relationships. These people have become a family to me, and I put what the Lord told me *in the back of my head.*

I remember He said three years, but hey, I don't want to keep thinking about that. I just want to do what God has given me to do to make the impact I can while God has me here.

As time progressed, it was like God kept reminding me, "Don't forget, three years. You only have three years. Don't you become too attached. Don't come to a place where when I tell you it's time to go, you can't release it. I am giving you three years, and after three years I am going to shift your life."

Well, three years came in May of this year and as soon as May came it was like there was a rumbling. It was as if everything kind of came to smack me dead in my face. Things started to look really shaky. Things started to look very unstable.

It was like, "Okay, it is time for you to go ahead and start preparing to transition. It is time for you to start putting people in place to lead. It is time for you to start allowing others to teach. It is time to start allowing others to share the word of God, *because you are not going to be here.*"

THE LORD WAS PREPARING ME

It appears within this last year I've been out traveling more than usual. Before, I didn't leave. I didn't travel as much, because as a pastor you need to be there with the people.

But this last year I traveled more than I've ever traveled before. It was as if the Lord was getting me prepared to be back out doing ministry *outside* of The Life Center.

When May came, we hit three years. It was June, then July, and the Lord said, "Okay, you have to go ahead and release this."

It was a couple of weeks ago, right when August hit, that I made the announcement to the church that the Lord has commissioned me to release this ministry, and I must release it into the hands of Pastor Nakia.

So, this is all fresh. It is all going on right now. I am *in* the transition as I write this. And yes, it is very, very sad.

I mentioned earlier about giving birth, I feel like a surrogate mother. One that has birthed this beautiful baby and has started to raise the baby, and I'm finally seeing the baby say his numbers, alphabets, and starting to hear the baby talk.

I am finally seeing this baby grow and develop, and right here when I'm seeing the baby grow, I have to let go and give this baby to someone else to raise.

I feel this is *my* baby. This is the baby that *I* birthed, but now I have to give this baby to someone else. I must believe, hope, and pray, who I give this baby to, they are going to be able to care for this baby, and love this baby, the same way that I love and care for them now.

Then to have to tell those babies that, "Hey, mommy has to go."

They have shared their heart with me, "Why are you leaving? We came here because of *you*. Your voice has been the one assigned to our life. We don't understand why you would leave. What are we going to do?" No, it has not been easy for any of us. We've all cried together.

LET PEOPLE KNOW YOU GENUINELY CARE

The natural side feels bad, because you never want anyone to feel like you're abandoning them or leaving them in the middle of the process. And so, if there were any regrets, it is the regrets of leaving people that I really, truly love. People that I have not just taken in as members, but who have become family to me.

It is the same feeling I had when I left my home church family. It is the same feeling I had when I left my husband and the church after all those years. I'm leaving with a feeling of grief.

It is leaving people and a place that I have built really great memories and relationships of. We have had good times together and that has probably been the *hardest* thing for me during this transition. Building those relationships was key to our rapid growth.

People have asked how we built the church so fast. I can honestly say that there was no strategy. I didn't have twelve steps to say, "This is how you grow your church." I just genuinely love the people. When people know you genuinely care about them and you build that trust, then that's when you can make a difference in someone's life.

I never separated myself from the people. My desire was, "I am here to serve you, I am here to help you. I am not here for you to serve me. I am here because I know I'm assigned to make your life better."

- If that meant I got in the trenches with you.
- If that meant I came to cry with you.
- If that meant you throwing up all over my clothes because you had a bad night drinking too much.
- If that meant I came to break up a domestic dispute between a husband and a wife.

Those were the things that I was willing to do. It was a denial of *me* to be a blessing to them.

When you're called to do ministry, you take on the example of Jesus Christ. He was called to those that were sick.

He said, *"The whole need not a physician. It's the sick people that do."*

I was willing to minister to the sick people, and unfortunately there are not many people that *really* want to minister to the sick. It is easy to be with people that have their stuff together, but – it takes work, it takes sacrifice, it takes patience. It takes you willing to give your money and your time. It takes you willing to lose rest.

My children sacrificed a lot, often because their mom was helping other people. It takes all those things to really, *again*, change people's lives for the better. I believe that that is what the difference is between me and many other leaders. Many will not make that sacrifice, and I do it with joy.

CHAPTER INSIGHT

- *Be careful of how much information you share with others about your transition.*
- *When you do share your story, be aware of how it will help others to see your struggle and your faith.*
- *Be honest: don't be afraid to share behind the scenes where everything does not look pretty.*
- *Watch for the signs of transition in your life.*
- *Let the people in your life know you genuinely care.*

Chapter Two

TRUSTING GOD WHEN YOU CAN'T TRACE OR TRACK HIM

God told Abraham, *"Hey, I need you to go to a land that I'm going to show you."* Which means just start walking, and as you walk, I'll reveal a little bit more to you *as you obey.*

In other words, He doesn't give you all the details. And it's the same thing for me.

God, I can't trace what you are doing. All you are telling me to do is release this ministry and you're going to lead me to something else. But He is not really telling me exactly what the something else is.

I have the idea; I'm still going to be ministering to people. I'm still going to be preaching the gospel. I'm still going to do all those things that I believe I'm called to do. But where I'm going to do it? How is it going to happen? *Who* are the people that I'm going to help?

Those are the things that I don't know. This is where I'm trusting God when I really can't trace Him, because I don't have all the specifics. All I know is at the end it's going to be good, but in the middle - I don't have a clue about what's going on.

$\mathcal{S}$TILL, I'M JUST TRUSTING GOD

- While I'm in the middle, while I'm in the gap, I'm trusting Him.
- While I'm waiting for more instructions, I'm trusting Him.
- While I'm waiting for Him to reveal to me the next phase, *I'm still trusting Him.*

Even though I don't trace all that's happening.

$\mathcal{C}$HARTER A NEW TERRITORY

With this move, He told me to release the ministry, and then He also said, "And get boxes and start packing up your house."

That is the next part. So, things are very uncertain, because I'm packing up my home. And that's the other thing - I not only love the church, I love my home. I love my neighborhood. I love my city. I love the school system.

I've been here *all my life*. So, to be told to get packing boxes and prepare to move? I already know that I'm relocating to another state. I know that. I know that I am not going to be here in Virginia.

I know that God is saying, "Your work is not just done with The Life Center, but your work is done here in this area, *period*. I'm getting ready to cause you to charter a new territory."

So again, I say, "I'm trusting you, God," but I can't trace Him because I don't know where I'm going. I just know it's not going to be here.

God Prepared My Children

And this causes a lack comfortability because as a parent you want to make sure your children feel stable. You want to make sure they feel secure. Their security is here. Their stability is here.

They've been in this school system for years. They excel in academics. Everybody kind of knows everyone else. It's a very beautiful town.

They've already gone through a transition when me and their father went through a divorce, and they went through that very smoothly. Now that I'm in transition, again, I don't want it to have a negative impact on them. The blessing is my children are very discerning. Just like God has prepared me to transition and God has prepared me to trust Him, it's as if God has prepared my children as well.

My oldest just transitioned to college, so all of this is happening all at once. I just dropped him off to college last week.

My second oldest, he's going to graduate next year. He's a senior now and he's going to be going off to college next year. So, it's going to be me and my daughter.

And so just me processing, my boys are getting ready to start having their own life and it's going to be just me and my baby in a strange land. We will have to meet different people. She will have to go to a new school. She will have to develop new friends, something that she's never had to do.

That's been a real concern of mine, but again, that is where your faith in God kicks in. You know, that, "Okay, God, you know what's best for me and I just don't believe that you will require me to leave something and send me somewhere that's not going to be better than what we left."

WHEN YOU MOVE, I'LL MOVE

I preached a message a couple of weeks ago, and this was the message *before* I announced the transition, '*When you move, I'll move*'. I was talking as the voice of God, "When you make the step, that's when I'm going to move for you."

Many of us have a practice of – and I'm including myself here – disobeying God or even half-obeying. And just so you know, that half-obedience is still disobedience.

WHEN YOU SEE SOMEONE ACTUALLY OBEYING GOD

- It looks as though they have lost their mind.
- It looks as though they are crazy.
- It looks as though they are operating in the flesh.
- It just looks like this cannot be God.

Obedience is not the popular thing. When we see obedience in demonstration, it looks strange. *It appears off.*

The Lord said to me, "Shavon, you have been waiting on me to do some things for you. You have been asking me to do some things *through* you. But know this, I am not going to move until you move."

And no, it won't be easy. You are going to be required to do the hard stuff. When God requires us to make moves, He is not going to give us anything that is easy. If it does not wrestle against your flesh, if it does not hurt, if it is not a sacrifice, then it is not of God.

He is not going to require something of us that we are willingly ready to let go of. He is going to require something from us that we don't want to do. He is going to require that thing that we have an affection to, an affinity to. He is going to require *that thing* that we love the most.

WHEN YOU OBEY GOD

Every time we obey His instructions, we are saying, "Okay, God, here I am. I am obeying you." *Me* releasing the church as I was instructed was one step in saying, "Okay, God, here I am. I am obeying you."

Then, as I released the church, I had an opportunity come to me the *very* next week. That opportunity took me to South

Carolina, ministering with such a beautiful congregation that I had never been to before.

I met this young man on an airplane, and he called his dad and said, "Dad, you've got to meet this lady."

At the time, I didn't know his dad was a pastor. The dad called me and said, "Hey, you don't know me, but my son sat beside you on the airplane and he gave me your information. I found you on Facebook and I need you here tomorrow."

This is what happens when you obey God. I just believe that every time you obey Him, then He releases what He has next in store for us.

When I obeyed my instructions and released The Life Center, I received my next instructions. I was told to get boxes and start packing up. So, I got the boxes.

Every time you make the steps, every time you walk in obedience, then God reveals a little bit more of His plan. So, the steps for me are to just obey His instructions to a *T.*

CHAPTER INSIGHT

- *Trust God while waiting on His instructions.*
- *God will always give you something better than what you already had.*
- *God is waiting on us to move. When we obey His instructions, then more of His plans for us will be revealed.*

Chapter Three

DEVELOP AN EAR TO HEAR THE VOICE OF THE LORD

You can develop an ear to hear the voice of the Lord the same way you do in a relationship with your spouse. Or the relationship with your children; the relationship with your family. The relationship with anyone in your life.

The more time you spend with them, the more you are in their presence, then the *more* you learn their ways. There will be times when they don't even have to say anything verbally. You just know what they want or need because you have spent time with them. You have learned how to live with them.

That's the same way it is when we are in relationship with God. The more we develop our relationship with God, where we're at one with Him, where we spend time with Him, where we commune with Him, when He speaks, ***we'll know His voice.***

When you hear a stranger's voice, you'll be able to discern the difference.

When I get married again, there will be no other man's voice that is going to sound like my husband's voice, because I'm in relationship with him. I know him in a way that I don't know anybody else.

It's the same thing when we're in relationship with God the Father. The more time we spend with Him, the more we are confident in knowing **this** is the voice of God.

I *know* it was the Lord that told me to release the church, *because I know what His voice sounds like.* I spend time with Him. As crazy as the instructions sound, I know it was His voice that said, "Go in and get some boxes and pack up." Again, because I am in relationship with Him, I know His voice.

When you're in the beginning or the infant stages of developing a relationship with God, you first must learn the character and the ways of God.

- Any voice that will make you feel condemned.
- Any voice that will make you feel less of a person.
- Any voice that will make you feel bitter or resentful.
- Any voice that will make you walk in guilt and shame.

This is a clear indicator that is **not** the voice of God.

$\mathcal{I}$NSTEAD, THE VOICE OF GOD IS

- One that will always build you up.
- One that will always inspire and strengthen.
- One that always makes you feel protected and safe.
- One, *most of all*, that gives you peace.

If you are in a place where you are feeling tormented, where you are feeling confused, where you are feeling frazzled, where you can't get your thoughts together, then that is a discerner. That is not the voice of God speaking. There are many voices in the land, but the voice of God will *always lead you-*

- To a place of peace.
- To a place of serenity.
- To a place of fulfillment.
- To a place where you don't feel that you are *missing* anything.

The voice of God will always complete you. His voice will leave you with nothing missing, nothing lacking, and nothing broken.

Listen for these indicators:

- What do those voices make you *feel* like?
- What do those voices lead you to do?
- Do the voices take you away from God's plan?

If the voice you hear takes you away from God's plan, it is not the voice of God.

There have been a lot of instances where I have moved in my flesh and I overrode what God said just because of fear.

- Fear of the unknown.
- Fear of the outcome.
- Fear of what people are going to think.
- Fear of what people are going to say.

I believe that when the three years came in May, I was supposed to release the ministry then. But because I have an affection for the people, because I now have an attachment to this place, I waited until August to do it. And because I waited, it probably caused more stress and more tension than what was necessary. I could have prevented that if I would have moved when the Lord told me to.

Back when I was a teacher in school, the Lord told me to release the job where I taught school. I taught school for seven years, and the Lord told me to release the job a couple of years in. I kept on teaching and I ended up getting laid off. It was as if the Lord forced me off the job because I didn't move when He told me to move. So, He shut the whole company down.

When the company closed, that's when I was receiving calls to travel and minister the gospel. I believe that if I would have released the job when He told me to, I probably would have been able to impact more regions. I probably would have been able to start a little bit earlier than I did in the ministry.

When I don't obey, I'm hard on myself. I'm one of those that beats myself up really bad. I'll be like, *"I messed up, I disobeyed."* When I disobey, I feel terrible. I feel like I have let God down. I will go through times where I say, "He is not going to use me because I didn't do what He told me to do."

I'm doing better with that and with really understanding the grace and the mercy of the Lord. I am very, very hard on myself. I don't want to mess up. I don't want to miss out on God. I don't want to misrepresent Him, so I'm very hard on myself with that.

I will be honest and say another thing that I have done different is I have always been transparent. I always share my stories of failure. I shared the stories about my divorce, and the things that I endured in my marriage. I have shared what I wish I would have done better. I have always been transparent with sharing.

I don't always get it right. There are sometimes that I feel weak. There are times I feel like I just want to lay a person out or I want to give them a piece of my mind. I don't always want to be the saint. I don't always want to act like a Christian.

There are moments where I want to be Shavon and beat somebody upside the head, but that there is not the right thing to do. But I share those moments, because again, I want people to know that I am human too, and if it wasn't for the grace of God, there is no telling where I would be. So, I freely share my moments of weakness and frailty.

HELD TO A HIGHER STANDARD

We as pastors, leaders, and preachers have been called to represent God and to speak on His behalf. We *are* held to a higher standard. I don't believe we'll ever get away from that. We can't live a life that is just reckless. We can't live a life where it's like, "Well, I'm human and I can do what I want to do."

There will be times where we can't do what we want to do. There will be things I want to do, but I can't do it *because* of the call on my life. *Because of who I represent.* Because God has pretty much placed me as a role model, as an example.

Again, I don't want to misrepresent Him. I am His representative, and if more leaders and more pastors and preachers, evangelists, missionaries - if we really take this call seriously, then we *will* be careful of how we live.

Does life happen with us, too?

Yes.

Are we perfect?

No.

Do we have some superpowers, or are we in a place where we will never fall or never make a mistake?

No.

I do believe that we must really do what the Bible says and walk circumspectly. Meaning, walk very carefully because we are living epistles. People are watching us. They are watching our lives. Watching our moves. Watching our conversations. Watching our relationships. We can be a stumbling block to somebody else if we do not carry what's on our life the right way.

*B*E AWARE OF GOD'S INSTRUCTIONS

We can be more aware of God's instructions by making a *personal* decision to do so. I believe that comes with *really* wanting to have a relationship with God and *not* just being religious.

It is a personal decision. Whether you have a title or not, whether you come from a church background or not. It is a personal decision to want to *know* God and to experience His love and His power. Letting Him *in*, letting Him come in and reign and rule.

Again, going back to spending time with Him –

- Spend time with Him in worship.
- Spend time with Him in prayer.
- Spend time studying His word.

It's in His word where you will learn who *He* is. It's His Word that explains His character. It's His Word that explains His nature. As you fall in love with the Word of God, you fall in love *with* God, because **He is the Word.**

And title or not, preacher or not, evangelist or not, or just somebody that is new to the faith, building that personal relationship is what is so important. That is what is going to sustain us in this evil world. In a time when people are so broken and looking for answers, that relationship with God is what keeps us in perfect peace.

That relationship with Him is what teaches us how to be good mothers, fathers, husbands, wives, neighbors. It is God that is the teacher. It is God that is the one that gives us the wisdom on how to really live a peaceful life in such a chaotic world.

CHAPTER INSIGHT

- *Build your relationship with God and learn his character so you can recognize His voice.*
- *Fear can hold us hostage while keeping us filled with unnecessary tension and stress.*
- *Have someone in your circle to support you in a positive way.*
- *It is a personal decision to become more aware of God's instructions.*
- *You will learn who God is in His Word.*

Chapter Four

DETACHING FROM THINGS YOU ARE ATTACHED TO

In order to detach from the things, you are attached to, you have to prepare yourself emotionally and mentally *first,* before you can physically walk away.

If you do not detox of that mentally and emotionally, your physical movement is not going to change the outcome - because that string is still attached. So, regardless of where you are physically, your mind is still in that same place.

When the children of Israel left Egypt, they were now out of bondage physically, but because their *mind* was still in bondage – here, God had freed them – but they were still acting as if they were slaves. They were still complaining and like, "Oh my God, wish we were back in the slave days."

They couldn't even enjoy their liberty because their mind was still in Egypt. I believe that the detox, the detachment, and the disconnection first must happen mentally and emotionally before you can really be totally free from it physically.

In making the transition or making that change to detach, there's *going to be* a lot of interference. I don't think you should always block out everybody's opinions or thoughts on it, because there are going to be people that really are trying to understand what you're doing.

For example, I can't just say, "Hey y'all, I'm leaving and I'm out of here." I at least need to try to explain why I'm leaving and what the *Lord* told me. Tell people what I feel God is positioning me *for*. Now, will everybody understand it? *Probably not.*

But I will consider outside influences –

- *Because* we've had a relationship.
- *Because* I've been in this place for a while.
- *Because* I've worked here.
- *Because* there have been opportunities given to me at this job, or at this place, or in this relationship.

Then it's just integral to at least explain that, "Hey, my season here is up. I appreciate what this season was *for* me, what it was *to* me, but now it's time for me to do something else. And I'm leaving," because of whatever the reason is.

Again, we're not responsible for their response. We cannot dictate how they are going to respond to our explanation. I *do* believe it's fair to at least try to share, to at least try to get those that you care about to understand where you are.

A Level of Revelation

You may not be aware you have more than one purpose or season. Not recognizing this can make it hard to let go. Make it hard to detach from the familiar and transition to the new that God has for you. I grew up in church, and this was not a teaching that I heard *at all*.

It was not until I grew into a relationship with God for myself and began to learn about Him and His ways. I would just go through scripture where I learned about transitioning and seasons, different times, and purposes. As we evolve, as times change, as we come into a greater knowledge and greater revelation, we can teach people from a greater level of revelation.

When we grew up, our pastors, our teachers, our parents, they were comfortable where they were. They've been married sixty years, "This is what I know, this is the life I live. I worked at my job until I retired. We've lived in this same house, our children were born here, and we raised them here and my grandchildren come here." Loyalty was everything to them, "You stay here, and you just make this work."

They were not so privy to this jump up and shift in the middle of life. Whatever they did, they got established, and they stayed established in that one place.

Today, things are different. We don't stay in the same house for forty years. We buy a house and know we will not live there long enough to pay the mortgage off because we may have to transition to our next season.

That next season may take us to a different part of town, a different city or state. Across the county. For some, even a different country. We understand, now, that company loyalty will not last thirty years or even until retirement age.

These are things we have had to learn on our own. This is not something that was passed down to us. And that is okay because you really can't teach something that you haven't experienced yourself.

Now, we can help those coming up behind us. Teach them what to look for. Teach them how to study the Word and discern the Voice of God for instructions.

CHAPTER INSIGHT

- *Prepare yourself mentally and emotionally first, before you detach physically.*
- *Do share about your plans, but remember we are not responsible for other's response to our transition.*
- *When you recognize you have more than one purpose or season, it will be easier to transition.*
- *In knowledge we can teach from a higher level of revelation.*

Chapter Five

OVERCOMING FEAR

Every time you have a victory, every situation where you come out as an overcomer, *it overrides the fear.* I always make the statement that, "My faith in God overrides fear."

So, even though my knees may be shaking, and believe me, my knees *are* shaking right now - I cannot tell you, *"Hey,* I'm *excited* about what is getting ready to happen!"

No, no, no!

I *am* scared. But, my faith in God overrides that fear. My faith in God is not going to keep me crippled and stunted in a place that I *know* I must move away from.

$\mathcal{F}$ALSE EVIDENCE APPEARING REAL

The natural side, or the carnal side, will say, "You've set yourself up to fail, you're going to get out there and you're going to flop. You're not going to be able to take care of yourself. You're going to struggle."

Those are all the things that fear is saying, but then my faith drowns *out* what fear is saying. Because I know what *God* has spoken. I believe that you overcome fear by your faith in the Lord.

- *That faith is **ignited.***
- *That faith is **strengthened.***
- *That faith is **increased.***

Every time you step out and *obey* God, then you can say, "*Man*, because I obeyed, look at what He has released to me. *Man*, because I obeyed God, look at what I was able to do."

$\mathcal{A}$ND -

- If I never obeyed, this would have never happened.
- If I never obeyed and walked away from the toxic relationship with my husband, I would have never experienced what was on the other side of my fear.

- If I never obeyed and walked away from the churches and people, I would have never been able to birth The Life Center.

Now, if I didn't obey and never walked away from The Life Center, I would never be able to birth what is getting ready to transpire in this next season. *My faith is pumped up every time I obey God and I see the outcome.*

I'm grateful He has sustained me. There has not been a situation where fear has overtaken me and caused me to not move. I'm grateful for that.

Fear has tried, of course. But your faith in God, even when you feel like you're going to fall, or you feel like it's going to overwhelm you or overtake you, that is when you start pulling on the strength of God, and that is when you remember that, "When I'm weak, that is when He is strong."

That is when you remind yourself of the Word and know that, "God is with me and no weapon is going to prosper, and He is going to keep my mind."

Those are the moments when I start speaking the Word back into myself. Those are the moments I start reminding myself of what God said. The more I speak the Word, the more I am built up.

I try not to allow moments for the enemy to talk to me and to talk to me for a long time. When you start listening to the enemy, *that's* when you allow fear to overtake you. I try not to give him opportunities to speak or to even talk long.

When he starts talking, I begin to do what the Bible says and command his words to come into obedience to what God said. I command the words of the enemy, the lies, to now come into obedience to what the Lord already spoke. *That is* whose words take precedence over my life.

WHEN YOU FEEL STUCK

That is when you have to fake it until you make it. I am saying there are times when you are going to have to get up. I remember when I was pregnant. Man, I did *not* feel good. I'm really tiny, so when I had my babies it would just take everything out of me. I would feel miserable.

I would still get up and put my little makeup on and put on my pretty clothes. Even though I didn't *feel* like it, I still went through the motions until it became my reality. Even though I didn't feel like moving.

Maybe you don't feel like moving forward, maybe you feel stuck, that is when you say, "You know what? I don't feel like it but I'm going to keep faking it until I feel something again.

I'm going to keep getting up. I'm going to keep singing songs and quoting the Word of God. I'm going to keep trying."

Pretty much, I am going through the motions right now, I'm going to be honest. But I'm going to keep doing it until I look up and what was once me going through the motions has now become my reality. When I look back, I see that I am not stuck anymore.

CHAPTER INSIGHT

- *Your faith will give you the strength to overcome your fear.*
- *Listening to the enemy is when you allow fear to overtake you.*
- *Give the enemy as little time as you can, or none at all.*
- *When you feel stuck, keep going through the motions anyway.*

Chapter Six

EMBRACING THE NEW

To embrace the new, you have got to go in with an open mind because where you are going, you have never been in *that* place before.

You should go in with *expectation*. You should go in *with anticipation!*

- What is going to happen?
- What is it going to look like?
- What is it going to feel like?
- What new people are involved in this new season?
- What new places will I see?
- What new opportunities will I have?

So that it is actually with a feeling of excitement that you go into the new, instead of fear. But it is also with that feeling of a little nervousness and maybe a little anxiety. Because again, you are going to a place that you have *never* been to before.

And it is not just you physically going to a new place, but you are going to a new place mentally. You are going to a new place emotionally.

You have to go to a new place spiritually because your faith has to be heightened for the new place. You are literally walking out believing what you cannot see. Hoping for something that is not really tangible, believing that what you imagine or what has been revealed to you is *really* going to manifest physically.

That first step is not just going in with an open mind, but going in with a sense of expectation, *because you don't receive anything if you never expect anything. You s*tart thinking of the things that you desire and then you get excited because of the Word of the Lord, for those that are led by God, we know that *God exceeds* our expectations. He does above what we can ever ask or think. *Go in with positive thoughts.*

My expectation is, I am going into a new land. I am going into a new territory. It is going to impact lives for the glory of God.

You go in with the things that, of course, you naturally desire knowing that whatever you naturally desire, God is going to exceed that.

He says that He does *above* what we can ever ask or think and so yes, my expectation is I am going to a new land. I am going into a new territory, and it is going to impact lives *for the glory of God*. I am going to be able to minister to all kinds of people from all kinds of backgrounds.

RELEASE HIM TO BE OUR FATHER

I feel as if sometimes we feel like if we asked for *too* much, we view it as being selfish or that it is not a sign of humility. God wants us to release Him to be our Father.

I use this example all the time - if Paris Hilton walks into a family hotel, she's not walking into the hotel with her head down. She's not even going in asking if there is a room available for her. She's pretty much going in and saying what she desires because of who her father is. She's walking in confidence.

She's walking into that hotel knowing that, "If I want to sleep on top of the roof, if I wanted to sleep in the basement, if I want to block the entire hotel, I can do that." *Why?* "Because my father *owns* this hotel."

And it is the same for us. Our Father, He *wants* to give us the gifts in accordance to His will because we are *His* children. Walk in confidence knowing *who* your Father is. Ask for what you want with the expectation and anticipation that your desires will be met.

There are no limitations to what He will do for you. There is no keeping count the number of times your desires will be answered.

Get Your Business in Order

The next step, realistically, is you need to get your business in order. *You must make preparation.* With transition, it is going to take resources and you must plan for your future. I don't believe you should just go out into the new without having things proper and in order.

If you know you are in a season of transition, it is going to take some savings. Saving of finances because you never know what money needs to be put out.

It is also going to be a matter of you being willing to sacrifice. There may be some things that you cannot do in a season of transition. There may be some things that you have to pull away from, some activities, and some enjoyments that you once had that you cannot do at the moment. Because again, you're preparing for transition. And transition incurs an expense.

And because you don't know what to expect, you want to make sure you have, not just enough, but you want to have *more than enough* because you never want to go into your new place having to struggle.

I believe preparing business-wise and making sure you close doors from that old chapter and that you close them the *right* way is going to make your transition easier. You never want to leave wrong. Doing these things correctly may prevent you from having regrets or even feeling a lack of confidence about your next steps.

For example, when you leave an old job, you don't just walk away from a job and say, "Hey, I'm gone." Some people do it, *but that's not the integral way.*

You give two weeks' notice when you leave an old job to give them time to find somebody else *and* to give you time to prepare for the new position.

This works the same way. You want to make sure as you're leaving *from* to go *to*, that where you are leaving *from*, you are closing those doors in an integral manner. You are making sure that if you are leaving a position, if you are leaving a place of influence, if you are leaving a place where people depend on you, that you are leaving a place where it doesn't fall to the ground. You are leaving a place where it still can be fruitful.

You never want your work and the things that you've done to go in vain.

So, that's another step, making sure that every door that is being closed from the old chapter is closed the right way. That doors are closed with integrity.

You want to have complete closure so that you really can walk into your new place - your new season - without any regrets, without any reservation, and without that *past* trying to pull you back because you did not close that door properly.

BE MINDFUL OF HOW YOU SPEAK

I'm very mindful of making sure when I speak of this new place and when I talk about the new transition, that I articulate it in a way where people around me become excited. I'm not sharing the fears or the uncertainties. I'm not sharing so much of my personal reservations that I may have because I don't want to put that fear into them.

For example, when I talk to my children, it is always from a standpoint of, "There is something so *amazing* that we're getting ready to walk into, we're getting ready to meet new people, make new relationships, and have an opportunity to see different cultures." When I put it that way to them, it causes them to be excited.

Don't want to walk around speaking about your next steps in tones of doubt and fear. Of course, that will just lead people to doubt and misunderstand. That is not how you honor God. Be *full* of confidence and faith. God is getting ready to do something wonderful in your life, share the news with the joy and gratitude He deserves.

RECOGNIZE TRANSITION

I believe many people are in transition and really don't realize what it is, and *that's* why they're so frustrated. They don't understand that's the reason why everything bothers them now, the very things that never bothered them before.

You know, you can *always* feel when it is time for you to change, when it is time for you to shift, or when it is time for you to *move* from a certain place, a certain people, a certain environment.

RECOGNIZE

- When what used to not bother you begins to bother you now.
- When what you were once comfortable with is now irritating to you.

- When what you once were willing to accept you have no tolerance for it now.

That is your sign. That is the indicator that, "Okay, I have now outgrown this particular season. I have now *maxed out* this particular place. I have now worn out my welcome." A lot of people don't know that those *are* the signs and the indicators of transition.

THEY JUST KNOW

- They are frustrated.
- They are tired.
- They are burned out.
- They have no joy.
- They are just going through the motions.

But they really can't pinpoint that, "You know what? I'm in *transition*."

AND THESE SIGNS

- The constant frustration.
- The feelings of confusion that everything is not lining up the way it should.

- It seems like things are not happening the way you thought they would happen.
- It seems like things are more of a drudgery than a joy.

You *really* don't understand that this is just the nudge. This is just the indicator that *now* is the time for you to move.

CHAPTER INSIGHT

- *Believe in what you cannot see.*
- *You don't receive if you don't have expectations.*
- *God will exceed your natural desires.*
- *Be willing to sacrifice in a transition.*
- *Close out the old with integrity.*
- *Learn to recognize when you are in transition.*

Chapter Seven

HAVING CONFIDENCE IN TAKING NEW TERRITORY

I just believe that our confidence comes from our faith in God, that our God knows what is best for us. He knows what *we* need more than we can even ask, more than we can even articulate it.

He knows.

So, our joy comes in - our confidence, our boldness - and our positivity comes from our faith in God. The confidence and authority that we have in this new season - it comes from our faith in God.

In knowing that, our God will *never* set us up to fail. In knowing that, if our God has pushed us and nudged us and told us that it's time to move, it's time to go, it's time to

transition, it's time to shift; ***then we need to get excited.***
Because He has something better *for* us.

"God, what is it you have up your sleeve now? If you're causing
me to now leave this place that I enjoy, that I have an affinity
with, to now transition from the people and the places where
I have been for years and you are now *commissioning* me to
move, then that only means you have something greater in
store. Because you will never have me to leave something and
not give me more than what I left."

But there will be times when the natural side comes in, *a
lot*. You may lose confidence in the transition you're about
to make. It still happens with *me*. There are days where I'm
very excited about what's getting ready to happen. You know,
the unknown. You can think of all kinds of things and tell
yourself, "Maybe it will happen like *this* or maybe it's going to
happen like *that*." *You get so excited.*

Then, there are days where I'm saying, "*Oh. My. God.* Maybe
this is *not* the right thing to do. Maybe I am making the *wrong*
decision."

It would be *easier* to just stay put. It would be easier to just
go back to everyone and just say, "You know what guys? I've
made a mistake. I'm going to stay here and we're going to just
continue doing what *we've* been doing."

When I have those moments where I'm almost backpedaling and I'm becoming unconfident, where I am almost becoming weak in that area of faith – that is when I now have to pull on the strength of God.

I just talk to Him and say, *"Okay, God. Shavon is weak, but now, I need your strength. Shavon is scared. I need you to remind me of who you are and your strength in me. I need it to be made perfect in my life. You know God, Shavon doesn't see what the future looks like. But God, I need you to make it clear to me. Bring me peace. Bring me revelation. Just remind me again that your thoughts towards me are going to be good."*

I believe that is when you start talking to your Father, just asking Him, again, to *reaffirm* who He is to you. For those that may not be comfortable talking to God or maybe you have not developed that relationship yet where you are comfortable having just a candid conversation with God, maybe it's best to start writing it out.

- Write out your feelings.
- Write out your fears.
- Write out your thoughts.

Then, after you write out all your thoughts and all your fears, then *now* combat what you wrote with the positive thoughts.

Say to yourself, "I may be fearful, but hey, if I let fear keep me, I will miss out on the now. I will miss out on this opportunity."

Then, start writing out the expectations and the things that you do desire for this next season. I believe if you begin to write out the things that you desire and the things that you expect, the things that you may have dreamed about, *that* is going to bring back that joy and bring back that confidence. That will bring back that excitement for the next place.

*I*T IS ABOUT THE CONNECTION

When we concern ourselves with how other people do things, we compare ourselves to others. I have heard people say they don't know how to pray, so they don't. Because they can't do it like others do.

Let us make sure that the *only* person we're measuring ourselves to or measuring ourselves by, *is God our Father.* If we measure ourselves by other people, then we will *always* feel unqualified and we will always feel like we are not seasoned enough. We will always feel that we're not experienced enough.

For example, there are people who pray, and they know just the right words to say. They sound just like they are just calling heaven down. But praying is not about a form.

The Bible says that the people have such a *form* of Godliness, but they deny the power of God. **Prayer is about the connection.** It's about the *sincerity*.

When I talk to new believers and new Christians and they say, "I can't pray like that. I don't know how to put my words together. My words kind of stammer. I don't even know how to say it. I don't know how to pray."

Well, I tell them *you* talking to God is no different than you talking to someone that you are in a relationship with. You talking to your Father in heaven is just like you talk to your child or talk to your natural father. It is like talking to your husband or talking to your wife.

It is talking to somebody that you love, and you want them to hear your heart. You want them to know your desires and concerns. Or you want them to do something for you.

The first thing you want to do is love on them. *That* is the first thing you do. You go to them saying, "Hey, I love you. I appreciate you. I thank you for who you've been."

That's the same thing we do with our Father. We love on Him *first*. We let Him know how much we can't live without Him.

Then, *after* you love on Him and talk to Him really good, sincerely, then you go into, "God, I need you. I need your strength. I need you to make me more like you. God, I'm not asking for things. I'm just asking for your heart. I'm asking for your nature." You go into it *that* way.

I believe that if you go in without a certain form or without a certain sound, but just going in out of *purity* of heart, you will touch heaven in a way that you would never ever imagine. Because a lot of the time, we will get focused on the length of the prayer, the loudness of the prayer, the certain word usages of the prayer.

But when you focus on *those* things, the prayer really doesn't have the impact it is supposed to have because it is just a form and it denies the power of God.

So, measure yourself *not by people*, but *measure yourself by God* and what God has already said about you.

PRAY WITHOUT CEASING

I am a firm believer in praying without ceasing. *I am praying all day long.* I guess I'm new school. I don't drop down to my knees all during the day. I'm praying while I'm in the store at TJ Maxx. I'm praying while I'm in the grocery store. I'm praying when I'm in my car going to get a hot dog.

My spirit is *constantly* seeking God for direction. Constantly loving on the Lord. Constantly asking Him to lead and guide me. Constantly asking for insight, for downloads, for direction.

When I wake up in the morning, I say, "Good morning Jesus." Then I'll ask Him, "Okay, what would you have for me to do today? God, I need you to lead me and guide me, order my steps. Because *you* said the steps of a good man are ordered by you and *everything* I do and say today, *I want it to bring you glory*. I don't want to do anything *without* your leading." That is my *everyday* conversation with the Father.

ℰVERY DAY I ASK HIM TO

- Lead me.
- Guide me.
- Order my steps.
- Order my thoughts.
- Keep my mind.
- Keep my tongue.
- Keep my spirit.

I believe that you are supposed to speak the word of God over your life. I believe that positive affirmations are definitely needed to sustain a *healthy and a whole life.*

I don't think everything positive comes from the Bible itself, but I believe that good positive talk is just healthy, period. You know you can find positive talk in a lot of places.

- Whether it comes from the Bible.
- Whether it comes from a book of inspiration.
- Whether it comes from a movie.
- Whether it comes from a TV show.

So, to me, any positive talk you find is good. You also have whatever you speak out of your mouth.

- I am happy.
- I am going to be at peace all day.
- I will not allow things to frustrate me.

Listen, God will speak through anything, anyone, any means, to get a message to us.

I've often said, "Facebook is prophesying today!" That's what I believe. Social media is happening to the heart of God.

CHAPTER INSIGHT

- *Our confidence and positivity come from our faith in God.*
- *Talk to your Father when doubt begins to sneak into your thoughts.*
- *Ask Him to reaffirm who He is to you.*
- *If you are uncomfortable speaking to God, communicate regularly by writing to Him about your fears and expectations.*
- *Only measure yourself to God our Father – not other people.*
- *Speak the Word of God over your life.*

Chapter Eight

Trusting that You are not in Trouble During Transition

Going back to how transition makes you feel, if you don't understand that this transition is a tool to get you to your next place, then you will *think* you're in trouble because it does not feel good.

It *feels* like trouble. It *looks* like trouble. It *looks* like everything is falling apart. It *looks* like, "Whoa, this is not making sense." This looks chaotic. *This was not in the plan.*

If you are not clear that this is one of the tools that is being used to prepare you for the next place - that this is not permanent, that this is just preparation – if you are not clear on that, then you will definitely think you are in trouble.

You will think –

- What did I do wrong?
- Am I being punished?
- Is my life taking a turn for the worse?
- Am I in trouble?

The peace comes in when you get a revelation that, "Nope, I'm not in trouble. *I'm just in transition.*"

Instead, Think

- This is being used to get glory out of my life.
- This season here is being used to place me in another position.
- This is being used to place me *in a better position.*
- This season here is being used to give me opportunity for a new audience.

Transition Is Just The Vehicle

I believe that the transition I'm in personally is just the vehicle, the tool, the motor, that God is using for me now to be able to impact more people. You know?

He is telling me, *"Okay, you have impacted the region where you are. You have left a mark. You have used your life to be a light. Now, I want to put you somewhere else and you are going to have a **greater** impact. I want to put you in a territory that needs to hear the Word of God. I want to put you in a place that needs to experience and feel the love of Christ. I want to put you in a place where people want your hugs and kisses and want you to love on them. I am preparing you to have greater influence."*

So, when you get the revelation, you finally realize, "Okay, no! I'm not in trouble. It *looks* bad, but it is *not* bad. It doesn't *feel* good, but it will work out *for* my good."

BE HONEST WITH YOUR FEELINGS

I feel when you are going through those moments where it doesn't feel good, like I'm going through moments *right now* where this does not feel good – you have to be real with yourself. I go through moments where I'm *sad. I'm crying.*

I don't want to overrule or even try to act like I don't feel that way. I believe that it's okay to say, "I don't like how this feels. I'm *hurt* that this has to happen to me. To us."

When people try to tell me, "It's going to be all right. You're doing what God told you to do."

"Yeah, I am." But I have to be honest with how I feel. I don't like it. I don't like how it's making *me* feel. I don't like how it's making *other* people feel. I don't like the uncertainty of it. But I have to embrace it.

When you have those moments - I say, *have the moments.* Cry. Kick. Scream!

And after you get done crying, wipe your face off and you say, "Okay. Now God, I got my tears out. I told you God, that this doesn't feel good. ***But I still trust you.*** I'm being honest with you, God. I don't like it, but I still trust you."

You know, Jesus had a moment when He had to go to the Cross. When He was in the Garden of Gethsemane, He's crying out to God. He's crying so bad that blood comes out of His forehead.

And he is saying, "God, why have you called me to do this? If there's any way possible, can you remove this cup from me? Can you remove this assignment? I don't want to go through this transition."

He's crying. He's like, this is not good. Then after Jesus had His moment, immediately He said, "You know what? But wait, not My will, but *your* will be done."

The human side is going to go through times where you don't feel good, but my thing is, you can't stay there. Have your moment. But get up and wipe your face.

You go ahead and you say, "Okay, this does *not* feel good. But it is going to work for my good. I am going to keep speaking it until what I speak becomes what I see. I have got to keep speaking it. I might not see it *yet*, but I am going to keep declaring it until what I see lines up with what is coming out of my mouth."

*T*HEY HAVE SEEN MY PAST JOURNEY

The few who don't question this transition I am going through is a very small percentage of people. They understand why I must obey. And the reason why they understand is because they have seen my journey already.

I believe it's because they've seen this walked out in my life. They have seen what I've gone through before. They have seen me come out better. They already know that if she says God told her, then God told her. *We trust that she hears the Voice of God.*

Those who question the transition are those that have not seen it. Or may not want to see how things have been walked out in my life. Maybe because of their own personal fears, they can't see it. Sometimes the fears people have about what you are going to do is based on their *own* personal experiences. And because *they* won't do it or because they are not *willing* to do it, then most certainly you are not going to do it.

They cannot see past how they see themselves. That is the majority of people in the world today. Because so many people live in fear and in doubt. So many want to stay comfortable and stay in a box, then they can't fathom when somebody else breaks out of that box. They can't perceive it. They can't conceive it.

The Bible says that to the carnal, to the one that lives in the carnal, things of the Spirit are foolishness to them.

OBEDIENCE IS NOT COMMON

That is where *this* book comes in. Obedience to God is not something that is common. It is not something that is popular. There is a very small percentage of people in my life *personally* that really, truly understand this journey. They understand so well that they can say behind my back, not just in front of me, but behind my back, "No, we know that God spoke to her and we're just excited about what is going to take place."

When you're in transition, be very careful not to say a whole lot. Be very careful who you allow to talk into your ear. Because if you are *not* careful, people will talk you right out of obeying what God has told you.

So, the way I have managed to deal with the negative people is, I don't give them an audience to say too much to me. Again, I'm human. Although a lot of the people don't mean to be bad. These are people that love me. These are my family members. These are the people that have been in my life for some time. It's not all bad intentions. Some of them are just talking from a place of concern and again, *it doesn't make sense to them.*

So, when you have a Word from God, when you have clear direction from God, you have got to be very careful that those you allow to *speak* in your ear are speaking the same things that God has already told you.

When it is the opposite –

- When it speaks doubt.
- When it starts to speak fear into my spirit.
- When it speaks negativity.

That is when I know I must close my ears to those voices. If I allow the negative voices, the nervous voices, the voices of doubt, and the voices that speak against what God said, then I am not going to move.

It is going to paralyze me because *now* their words are going to have more weight than what God's words are for my life.

I'm at a funny, little place right now. I don't really allow myself to even be out to do a lot of talking or listening to a lot of people. I'm in a sensitive spot right now. There are only a few people I allow to share with me.

So, be careful who you allow to speak in your ear. Not everyone will understand your assignment and your transition will not always make sense.

CHAPTER INSIGHT

- *Think and connect with how your transition makes you feel.*
- *Your transition is a tool for your next place.*
- *Have your moment when you need to. If it doesn't feel good, be honest with yourself.*
- *Be careful with how much information you share with negative people.*

Conclusion

TRANSITION CORRECTLY

Transition is never an easy thing. Yet when you hear the voice of God, know that you must be obedient and move when He says move. Though fear may be present, you must put your faith into action and go forward. Keep in mind and consider that you are leaving people, places, or things that are still very dear to you; therefore, it is important to prepare yourself emotionally and mentally because transition can often make you feel like you are going through a grieving season.

In your season of transition, you are leaving and moving from some things that you have an attachment to. You must prepare your mind and emotions for that loss, because it's going to be different.

Things are not going to be the same anymore. There are people you used to talk to and people you saw often, that will no longer be in your life. There are places you regularly went to that you will no longer see. Maybe it was the office building where you worked. Maybe it was a favorite restaurant. Maybe it was a shopping center. These are familiar places. You're used to doing things a certain way. You're used to going about your life in a particular rhythm. Now, your whole life is changing.

When entering this season, I believe you must first make a change to your mindset and make sure you close the doors from the old place with integrity. Already knowing that you are going into a new territory and the way you used to do things will no longer work as you move forward. You can't go into this new thing doing things the old way. You can't have new wine and continue to put it into old bottles. You can't drive this new freeway and expect to get to the old destinations.

Prepare yourself mentally, physically, and spiritually. This is now the time to pull on God like never before - Because you are so vulnerable. Because you are in a place of uncertainty. Because you are grieving.

This is the time where you commune with God, seek Him for direction, and keep a keen ear to His voice. The more you talk to Him, the more you commune with Him, then the more you will develop an ear to hear Him. *And to know that it's Him talking to you.*

Now is also the time to strengthen your prayer life with the Father. Write out even your most personal plans. Write out the goals and vision you desire. What is it that you desire to accomplish? Write it out.

The Bible says, "Write out the vision and make it plain." You don't want to go into your new season without a plan. If you don't have a plan, *then you are planning to fail.*

Being prepared before you fully arrive will lessen your struggles. You don't want to move and have things worse than what you left. Make sure that you have everything in place before you physically move to the next place.

In transition, make sure that you have an idea of what it is you are going to do in this new place. Through studying the word and prayer, you can have faith and gain confidence that everything will fall into place knowing that all things will work together for your good in your new season. As you move, you will begin to see things manifest and align with what He has already shown you. Most importantly, seek God and continue to trust and obey Him even when it makes you look stupid knowing that nothing you do for the Lord is ever useless.

To Transition Correctly

- Close the door on the old with integrity.
- Prepare yourself mentally, spiritually, and emotionally.

- Make sure your business and finances are in order.
- Write your plan.
- Keep moving to have your next steps revealed.

Tools

and

Resources

$\mathcal{S}$CRIPTURES TO DISCOVER GOD'S CHARACTER

I love the Word of God, and it's like every time you open it, you learn more of Him!

Psalm 138:6-8

I love the scripture where He says, "I will perfect that which is your concern," where He talks about however you may be hurting, whatever you may be disappointed about, I'm going to perfect that. I love you so much that whatever makes you hurt, I'm the one that's going to heal that.

1 Peter 5:7

Another scripture says, "Cast your cares upon me, because I'm the one that cares for you."

Matthew 11:28-30

"Lay down your burden and just take on my yoke, because my yoke is easy." What I have for you to carry, it's not burdensome, it's not heavy, it's not going to wear you out, it's not going to make you feel bad. "My yoke is easy, and my burden is light."

Jeremiah 29:11

I think about how much He loves me and His plans for me, and I go to Jeremiah that says, hey, I know it may not look good, but "my plans for you, they're not evil." Everything that you may be facing now, it might not feel good, it's just preparatory, because my plans for you are good, they're not evil. I am setting you up, I have an expected end for you, and it's going to all work for your good.

Romans 8:28

I go over to Romans, and it talks about "everything is going to work for the good of them that love God and for those that are called according to His purpose." So even when it doesn't feel good, it's going to work for your good.

COMMUNICATE WITH GOD

Write down your fears and expectations to share with God.

_____

_____

_____

_____

_____

_____

_____

_____

_____

_____

_____

_____

About the Author

Pastor Shavon Sellers, a native of Norfolk, Virginia, is a mighty woman of God who demonstrates God's love to others throughout the country. Her love for God and her commitment to serving helping others is evident through her lifestyle of service. Her walk is evident in her obedience and willingness to trust God in all things. Her full-time mission is to ignite a renewed passion for God in the hearts of men and women everywhere.

Pastor Sellers holds a Bachelor of Science degree in Music Education from Norfolk State University. Professionally, she has impacted the lives of children as a teacher in the state of Virginia in the Norfolk and Newport News Public School systems. Above all her accomplishments, she considers raising Godly children her primary purpose. As a mother of two sons and a daughter, she firmly believes that the best way to raise successful children is to actively model what it means to walk in love and integrity.

Sought after nationally to minister God's Word in conferences and retreats, she has also authored two powerful books, You are the Prize and Empowering Moments 21 Day Devotional and is currently working on her third publication. In addition to being an author, Pastor Sellers started her musical journey with the release of her CD single "Supreme God", produced recordings of Prayers for Intercession, and a Life After Divorce DVD to help others deal with traumatic experiences.

In 2012, Pastor Sellers founded Shavon Sellers Ministries, whose vision is to spread the love of God, ignite the passion of God in others throughout the Kingdom, and to assist others in carrying out their God-given assignments and fulfill purpose. The mission of Shavon Sellers Ministries is to provide services such as vision casting development, leadership development, church planting, ministry coaching, and mentorship. As a subsidiary of Shavon Sellers Ministries, Pastor Sellers has also launched the Shavon Sellers Partnership Program as well as the Empowering Moments Mentorship for men and women.

In 2015, Pastor Sellers founded The Prize Foundation, an organization supporting communities in different areas and empowering women. Her desire is to teach life skills, job readiness and ultimately spiritual awareness, and to assist in the holistic recovery of those who have been hurt and abused.

Being led of the Holy Spirit, in May 2016 after the leading of the Lord Shavon Sellers planted The Life Center in

Chesapeake, VA where the vision is to be the voice and hands on the earth that will help people find their way back to God and begin a new life through Him. On November 19, 2017, Pastor Sellers was officially installed as Pastor of The Life Center in Portsmouth, VA. During her tenure as Pastor, it was her desire to revive believers, reach lost souls and connect people with the Savior. In August 2019, God required Pastor Sellers to release her role as Pastor of The Life Center and she is now fully committed to traveling to spread the gospel and reaching and empowering others through Shavon Sellers Ministries.

Connect with Shavon Sellers Ministries on Social Media:

https://www.facebook.com/iamshavonsellers/
https://www.instagram.com/shavonsellers/
www.shavonsellers.org

CPSIA information can be obtained
at www.ICGtesting.com
Printed in the USA
BVHW031626221219
567481BV00003B/5/P